Foreword

In our society, there are four things that draw attention: religion, war, politics, . . . and sports. Sports is by far the most democratic of the four. When held apart from religion, war, and politics, sports is at its best. It doesn't have a color code, an economic code, or a gender code. Success or failure is clear and un-debatable: there's no gray area, no room for interpretation, you either are or you aren't. Often the honor of sports is, quite simply, in the competition. This is the power of sports in essence: its ability to raise a white flag and bring people of all backgrounds together.

The athletic arena is a significant platform on which great societal steps are taken. Black athletes helped pave the road during the civil rights movement of the 1960s; the reverence and awe with which America viewed Jackie Robinson and Muhammad Ali echoed the nation's cries for equality. Woman fought for equal treatment and the passage of Title IX; they quickly found the uncharted territory of collegiate scholarships and professional sports.

Nothing creates a sense of community in America like sports. Anyone with heart and motivation gets an all-access pass. The power of sports to include and welcome everyone from different cultures, religions, genders, and age is palpable.

Sports allows us to feel success through another's achievement. Athletes have a unique ability to inspire, motivate, and exhilarate. Through their actions, athletes touch the hearts and lives of all Americans. Herein lies the hidden message of sports: sports inspires us individually and as a nation to be better.

William F. "Bill" Russell

Russell at the University of San Francisco, 1956

Gibson wore this traditional tennis outfit in the 1957 Wimbledon tournament.

The American underdogs stunned the world when they exploded out of their ro
upset victories at the 1980 Lake Placid Olympics. In the game dubbed the "mi
Olympic hockey team led by coach Herbert Brooks defeated the Soviet Union.
Finland to win the gold medal, a dramatic triumph that proved a powerful ren

"Do you believe :

— Al Michaels, ABC newsca

Firsts

In 1954, in Oxford, England, British medical student Roger Bannister (b. 1929) became the first person to run the mile in under four minutes. His time: 3:59.4. In a post-war world where technology was beginning to reign, Bannister's feat was viewed as an exhilarating testament to the power of the human body and spirit.

Bannister wore this jersey in his epic 3:58.6-minute victory against John Landy, the world's second sub-four-minute miler, at the Commonwealth Games at Vancouver a few months later.

In 1926 American swimmer Gertrude Ederle (1906–2003) captivated the world as the first woman to swim the English Channel. Ederle symbolized the modern woman with her strength and independence.

Ederle designed these watertight leather and rubber goggles for her 14 1/2-hour, 35-mile swim in the Channel's frigid, choppy waters.

Jack Roosevelt "Jackie" Robinson (1919-1972), the first African American to play in the modern major leagues, became a symbol of an individual's ability to effect change. Beginning in 1947, when he joined the Brooklyn Dodgers, Robinson encountered praise and prejudice throughout his 10-season career. Handling both with wisdom, he recast the racial attitudes of many Americans.

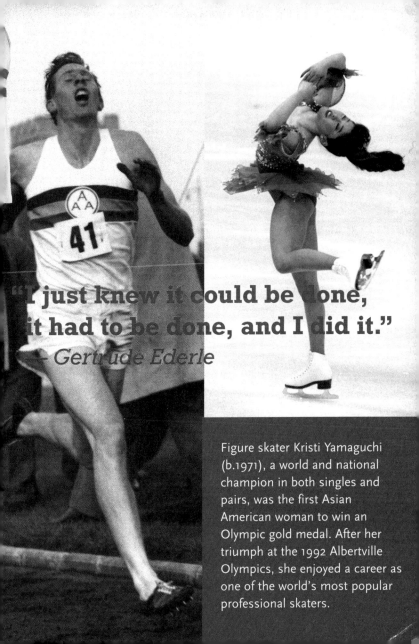

"I just knew it could be done, it had to be done, and I did it."
— *Gertrude Ederle*

Figure skater Kristi Yamaguchi (b.1971), a world and national champion in both singles and pairs, was the first Asian American woman to win an Olympic gold medal. After her triumph at the 1992 Albertville Olympics, she enjoyed a career as one of the world's most popular professional skaters.

Olympians

The Olympic Games, always about records, removed barriers, too, as they grew from elite amateur athletics in 1896 to today's international sports extravaganzas. Barriers to participation fell over time as more athletes demanded to take part, forcing the inclusion of women, additional countries and ethnic groups, and different sports.

Record setting became a matter of national as well as individual pride. American athletes have broken both records and barriers with their prowess. Their wins were often interpreted as victories for their nation, race, sex, or even equipment manufacturer. Usually, their losses remained their own.

miracles? Yes!"

in division with a series of
ice," the rag-tag U.S.
ericans went on to beat
America's Cold War distress.

"Faster, high

— motto of the O

Olympians

The modern Olympics, first held in Athens in 1896, emphasized strict amateurism and participation over winning. Some 250 male athletes from 14 nations competed in 43 events in nine sports. The Games have not only endured for more than a century, they have flourished. In the 2000 Sydney Olympics, more than 10,000 men and women from 200 nations participated in 300 events in 28 sports.

Figure skater Brian Boitano (b. 1963) captured four U.S. championships, two world championships, six World Professional championships, and one Olympic gold medal during his competitive career. Excelling in one of the few Olympic sports that can lead to professional performance, he has been a celebrated pro skater for many years.

Boitano wore these Harlick skates in his long program at the 1988 Calgary Olympics. The boot company added the American flags for good luck.

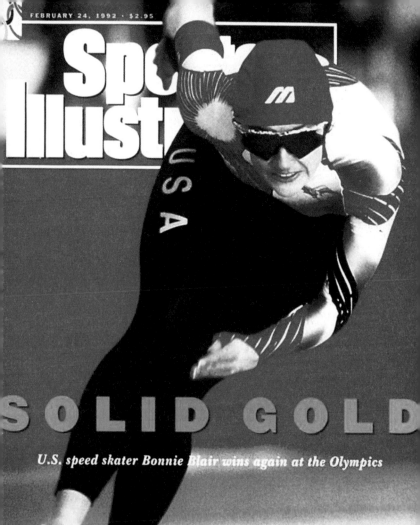

FEBRUARY 24, 1992 · $2.95

Sports Illustrated

SOLID GOLD

U.S. speed skater Bonnie Blair wins again at the Olympics

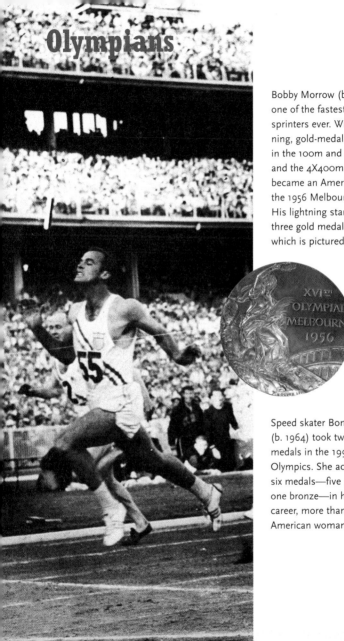

Olympians

Bobby Morrow (b. 1935) was one of the fastest American sprinters ever. With his stunning, gold-medal performances in the 100m and 200m dashes and the 4X400m relay, Morrow became an American icon after the 1956 Melbourne Olympics. His lightning starts earned him three gold medals, one of which is pictured here.

Speed skater Bonnie Blair (b. 1964) took two gold medals in the 1992 Albertville Olympics. She accumulated six medals—five golds and one bronze—in her Olympic career, more than any other American woman.

Every participant in the 1896 Olympic Games received a bronze medal designed by Belgian sculptor Godefroid Devreese (1861-1940). The practice of awarding gold, silver, and bronze medals began in 1904.

Gymnast Dominique Dawes (b. 1976) was the first African American to earn a place on the U.S. gymnastics team and the first to win an individual Olympic medal in women's gymnastics. At the 1996 Atlanta Olympics, she was a member of the team that brought home the first U.S. gold medal for gymnastics. Dawes won an individual bronze for the floor exercises. She has also won 15 national gymnastics championships since 1983.

r, stronger"

pic Games

MASTERS TOURNAMENT
AUGUSTA NATIONAL GOLF CLUB
WINNER ARNOLD PALMER 1958-60

With his charisma and amazing talent, golfer Arnold Palmer (b. 1929) injected new excitement into the game. He received this trophy after his second (of four) Masters Tournament victory in 1960. It depicts the Augusta (Georgia) National Golf Club, a private club that barred black members until 1990 and still barred women members more than a decade later. Recent controversies over its policies expose ongoing barriers to equal participation in sports that remain to be broken.

Mia Hamm (b. 1972) tra— formed women's soccer popular pro sport. After the national soccer team 15, she achieved two wo— championships and, wit— college team, four NCA— pionships. Hamm led th— team to a gold medal at 1996 Atlanta Olympics, time women's soccer w— included. Her team also silver at the 2000 Sydne— Olympics. Considered th— world's best female socc— er, Hamm was a foundir— ber of the WUSA, the wc— pro soccer league, and p— for the Washington Free—

Sports
Illustrate

APRIL 2, 1962   25 CENT

THE MASTERS

ARNOLD PALMER

Game Makers

Top competitors are pacesetters determined to make their mark on their sport. These are the athletes other sportsmen and sportswomen measure themselves against, the ones who set records and raise standards of play. Their challenging careers and great moments of achievement are electrifying events exalted by the media and savored by fans. Game makers become legends through their achievements; they are athletes who leave their sport transformed.

"I loved playing pro football. I loved it. It was my heart and soul and my mind"

— Terry Bradshaw

Quarterback Terry Bradshaw (b. 1948) took the Pittsburgh Steelers from last place in 1969 to Super Bowl victories in 1974, 1975, 1979, and 1980.

"Hammerin' Hank" Aaron (b. 1934) broke Babe Ruth's 71-home-run record in 1974 while playing for the Atlanta Braves. His accomplishment was not universally cheered, however. A he neared Ruth's record, racist hate mail increased. Two years later, as a Milwaukee Brewer, Aaron hit his 755th home run, a record that remains unbroken.

Sandy Koufax (b. 1935) used this glove during a celebrated career with the Los Angeles Dodgers that included pitching a perfect game and four no-hitters. Koufax successfully challenged Major League Baseball's practice of scheduling games on Jewish holy days.

More than Sports Champions

The rare athlete is a true hero. Although many are thrust into the limelight, a few take their heroic roles seriously. By taking on the burdens of others, a champion becomes the people's representative, their spokesperson, their beacon of hope. The performances of these valiant sportsmen and sportswomen, in and out of athletics, changed attitudes and conditions, and strengthened their communities.

Considered one of America's finest athletes, Jim Thorpe (1887–1953) was an Olympic track star and professional football and baseball player. He helped organize the forerunner of the National Football League and served as its first president. Of part Native American descent, Thorpe tirelessly promoted Indian causes.

This silver trophy for first place in a 1914 foot race at the Bronxdale (New York) Athletic Club is one of the hundreds of trophies Thorpe won over the years.

Roberto Clemente (1934–1972) first played pro baseball in his native Puerto Rico. He played 18 seasons for the Pittsburgh Pirates, from 1954 until his death in an airplane crash while delivering supplies for earthquake victims in Nicaragua. With a record of more than 3,000 hits, Clemente is remembered as a baseball great and an untiring humanitarian.

Clemente's 1960s batting helmet represented a new focus on baseball safety. After six major and minor league batters were killed by fastballs, Major League Baseball mandated the use of protective headgear.

Tim Brauch (1974-1999), who spun his childhood obsession with skateboarding into an international championship career, used this Santa Cruz skateboard in the 1998 Vans Triple Crown Championship. The skateboarding champion also designed boards and clothing for the unique skateboarding culture.

"If you ever get a second chance in life, you've got to go all the way."
— *Lance Armstrong*

Lance Armstrong (b.1971), a cancer survivor dubbed the "Healing Cyclist" for his work for cancer awareness, won the gruelling Tour de France in 1999, 2000, 2001, 2002, 2003 and 2004. His victories wiped away seemingly insurmountable physical and psychological barriers.

In 2002, Armstrong wore this yellow jersey, which signifies the race leader, in the Tour de France, the most prestigious cycling race in the world.

Barrier Removers

Inventive Americans removed barriers to sports by extending opportunities for everyone. As sports became a hallmark of the American way of life, people demanded a chance to play and excel. Inventors refined or invented equipment to make sports safer, easier, and more accessible. Others proved that barriers could be overcome by the mind, muscle, and miracles.

Engineer, inventor, and businessman Howard Head (1914–1991) revolutionized the ski and tennis industries. He made the first metal laminate skis in 1950 and introduced a metal tennis racket at the 1969 U.S. Open. His innovative Prince tennis racquet was 20 percent larger than the conventional racquet, but its "sweet spot" (the effective hitting area) was four times larger.

Owen Churchill (1896–1985) transformed scuba diving and snorkel-
ing with his ribbed rubber swim
fins. In 1940 Santa Monica life-
guards were the first to use his
invention for rescue work.

RECREATION

$2.00

November/December 1983 Volume 9 Number 4

The
US Tennis
Championships

By introducing a lighter and more maneuverable wheelchair, Marilyn Hamilton
(b. 1949) and her Quickie Wheelchair Company made tennis and other sports
more accessible to athletes with disabilities. Using her own design, Hamilton,
a paraplegic, twice won the U.S. Women's Open Wheelchair Tennis Tournament.
In addition to her tennis titles, Hamilton has won two silver medals in the
Paralympic Games and is the six-time National Disabled Ski Champion.

During his years as a Cleveland Browns running back, Jim Brown became one of the highest-paid and most-honored NFL players time. In 1963, Brown became the first player to rush over one m single season. In his nine pro seasons he averaged 1,368 yards 104.3 yards a game, and 5.2 yards a carry. The handsome player football for Hollywood where he starred in dozens of films. Late Brown found his most important role fighting for racial equality

Superstars

Brazil[...]
tion, h[...]
Cup m[...]
he led[...]
ity of [...]
sport.[...]

Pelé's N[...]

Soaring above the competition, Michael "Air" Jordan (b. 1963) transcended basketball. This superstar's stellar performance, charismatic personality, and marketing genius made him a magnet for advertisers, the media, and fans. Before turning to coaching, Jordan earned the NBA's most valuable player award five times and won six championships in his 13 seasons with the Chicago Bulls. Jordan used #23 for most of his career; after a brief retirement to play baseball, he returned to the Bulls as #45 but soon switched back to #23.

Superstars

Athletes of surpassing ability and charisma—superstars—
radiate an appeal that transcends sport. Through the media,
popular culture, and commerce, these larger-than-life icons
command worldwide attention. As athletes they inspire
imitation. As super-celebrities they capture the public
imagination. As historical figures they dramatize the values
and dilemmas of their times.

"The game is my life."
— Michael Jordan

layer Pelé (b. 1940) elevated soccer to international recogni-
nenomenal ability brilliantly showcased on televised World
es. Pelé ended his career with the New York Cosmos, which
ie 1977 world championship. His legacy is the global popular-
r among men and women as an amateur and professional

Cosmos Jersey

SPORTS
ILLUSTRATED

SEPTEMBER 26, 1960   25 CENTS

PRO FOOTBALL

Secrets of a Fullback
by Jim Brown

In his 1974 "Rumble in the Jungle" in Zaire, Muhammad Ali (b. 1942) pummels George Foreman. His victory proved his claim that he was "the greatest." Among his 21-year career highlights are an Olympic gold medal (1960); his first heavyweight title (1964); his refusal to serve in Vietnam on religious grounds for which he was stripped of his title (1967); his vindication by the Supreme Court (1970); his recapture of the title (1974); his loss and unprecedented third title recovery (1978); his retirement (1981); and his heroic battle against a debilitating illness. During these years, Ali became a media star and a symbol of courage, independence, and determination.

Ali wore this robe to the "Rumble in the Jungle" and autographed it in 1976.

Sonja Henie (1912–1969), one of the world's most famous figure skaters, popularized the sport with her spectacular spins, theatrical performances, and short skirts and white skates. After her unequalled amateur successes, the Norwegian American skater combined athletics and glamour in traveling ice shows and starring roles in 10 Hollywood films.

Superstars

"I am the greatest!"
— Muhammad Ali

Babe Ruth (1895–1948) revolutionized baseball with his flamboyant style and an amazing record of more than 40 home runs in each of 11 seasons. His record 714 home runs stood for four decades, surpassed only by Hank Aaron. The extravagant champion used radio, advertising, and movies to become the most famous athlete of his time.

Before the 1920s, batters rarely hit balls out of stadiums, and balls were seldom autographed. Ruth regularly drove balls into the stands, and fans lined up to have him autograph them. In 1926, as a gift to a sick child, the team trainer had this ball signed by Ruth and 26 other New York Yankees.